A First Look
THE
BIBLE

Lois Rock

Illustrated by Carolyn Cox

Educational consultant: Margaret Dean

A LION BOOK

Bible passages mentioned in this book:

1   Genesis, chapter 1 to chapter 2, verse 4.

2   Genesis, chapter 6, verse 9 to the end of chapter 9; also Genesis, chapter 17, verses 1 to 8; also Luke, chapter 1, verses 67 to 79.

3   Psalm 78.

4   Exodus, chapter 20, verses 1 to 17.

5   Isaiah, chapter 40, verses 1 to 11.

6   Proverbs, chapter 15, verse 1, and chapter 11, verse 25; also, Ecclesiastes, chapter 7, verse 5.

7   Psalms 148 and 42.

8   Psalm 16.

9   Matthew, chapter 28.

10 Acts, chapter 12 and chapter 27.

11 Colossians, chapter 3, verse 12.

12 Psalm 119, verse 105.

13 2 Timothy, chapter 3, verse 15.

Text by Lois Rock
Copyright © 1994 Lion Publishing
Illustrations copyright © 1994 Carolyn Cox

The author asserts the moral right
to be identified as the author of this work

Published by
Lion Publishing
4050 Lee Vance View, Colorado Springs, CO 80918, USA
ISBN 0 7459 3749 7

First edition 1994
First paperback edition 1997
10 9 8 7 6 5 4 3 2 1 0

Library of Congress CIP Data applied for

Printed and bound in Singapore

Contents

What is the Bible?   Introduction

Questions   1

Promises   2

Family stories   3

Rules   4

Reminders   5

Advice   6

Songs   7

Prayers   8

Life stories   9

Adventures   10

Letters   11

Light in the dark   12

Answers   13

Introduction
What is the
Bible?

The Bible is a book that is special to Christians. It is a collection of many different books—rather like a bookshelf with lots of different books in a row.

The books in the Bible were written by many different people at different times between 2,000 and 3,000 years ago.

The oldest books tell of the promises God made to a man called Abraham, and about how God looked after Abraham's descendants—the nation called Israel. These old books have always been special to the people of Israel. Today they are still the holy books of their descendants, the Jews.

Christians call these books the Old Testament.

The rest of the books in the Bible were written by the first people who believed in Jesus Christ—the first Christians.

Christians call these books the New Testament.

The Old Testament was written in Hebrew and the New Testament in Greek. Today, the books have been translated into the language you speak. Other people, in countries all over the world, have a Bible translated into their language too.

What is special about the Bible is that the writers all knew God—they loved and obeyed him.

● They wrote about the things God had told them.

● They wrote about the things God had done, so that other people would know what he was like and how he wanted them to live.

This book explores some of the most important things you will find in the Bible itself.

1 Let's look at
Questions

Why?
It's at the start of so many questions.
Why is the sky blue?
Why do birds sing?
Why do bees sting?
Why are people sometimes kind
and sometimes cruel?
Why were you born?

Genesis, the first book in the Bible,
begins with a story
about why the world is.
It says that God made the world
when there was nothing there:
he made earth and sky,
sun, moon and stars,
land and sea.
He made living things:
trees and flowers of all kinds,
fish, birds, and animals.
And he made people
to live in his world and to take care of it.

God looked at everything he had made, and he was very pleased.

From the first chapter of Genesis, the first book in the Bible

The Bible explains why the world exists: because God made it just as he wanted.

2 Let's look at
Promises

If you make a promise you must keep it.

God has made promises.

Long ago, God sent a flood to get rid of all the badness in the world. Afterward, God promised never to flood the world again. The rainbow is the sign of his promise.

Years later, God chose the nation called Israel to be his special people. God promised to take care of them.

There was one more promise. From the beginning, people had chosen to do bad things. It meant they could not be friends with God. The wrong they do makes them unhappy.

God promised to send someone to put things right.

Let us praise the Lord,
the God of Israel.
He has come to the help of his people
and has set them free.
He has sent someone to rescue them . . .
as he promised long ago.

From the book Luke wrote, in the New Testament

Christians believe that God kept that promise by sending his own son, Jesus, to show people how they could be friends with God again.

The Bible tells people about God's promises to care for them and for the world.

3 Let's look at
Family stories

Can you remember when
you were really little?
All those memories
are the first part
of the story of your life.
It is just a little part
of the story of your family.

The Bible tells the story
of a family that became a whole
nation: the people of Israel.
It's a true story
and it began nearly 4,000 years ago.
God gave them a land to live in
and told them what they must do
to be happy.
And whatever they did—in good times and bad—
he still loved them.

*We will tell our children
and our grandchildren
about God's power
and the great and wonderful
things he has done.*

From Psalm 78, in the Old Testament

**The Bible tells the story of God
and his people, and it shows
how much God loves everyone.**

4 Let's look at
Rules

When you have rules
you know what you can do
and what you can't do.
Good rules
are there to help you,
and they make you
feel safe.

The Bible says that
God gave his people rules
that told them how they
should live
in order to be happy.
There were ten great rules—
the Ten Commandments.

I am your God: you must worship only me.
Do not worship anything or anyone else.
Never use my name as a swear-word.
Keep one special day of the week for resting.
Show respect for your father and mother.
Do not kill.
Husbands and wives,
keep your special love
for each other only.
Do not steal.
Do not tell lies.
Do not be jealous of what other people have.

From chapter 20 of the book called Exodus, in the Old Testament

**The Bible gives God's rules for
living a really happy life.**

5 Let's look at

Reminders

So you forgot
what you were supposed to do.
Why didn't someone remind you
how important it was
to do as you were told?

The people of Israel kept forgetting
that God had chosen them.
They forgot his rules.
God sent special people—
the prophets—to warn them,
to remind them that disobeying God
would only lead to unhappiness.
The warnings were true:
the people lost battles
and were captured by their enemies.
God sent many prophets
to remind the people
that he still loved them,
still cared.

God says this:
*"Encourage my people;
tell them the good news
that I am coming to take
care of them
as a shepherd takes care
of little lambs."*

**From the book written by a prophet called
Isaiah, in the Old Testament**

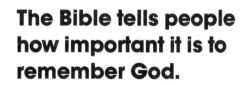

**The Bible tells people
how important it is to
remember God.**

6 Let's look at
Advice

Good advice is really helpful.
When you don't know what to do,
when you feel confused or worried,
it's nice to have someone
to make things clear.

The Bible has whole books
of good advice
for people who want to live in
the best way.
They talk about everything—
big and little—
that happens in life.

*A gentle answer
can stop someone
being angry.*

**From a book of wise sayings
called Proverbs, in the Old
Testament**

*If you help others
you will be helped.*

Another of the Proverbs

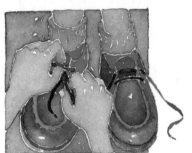

*It's better to have wise people tell you off
than to have silly people
say how great you are.*

**From a book of wisdom, called Ecclesiastes,
in the Old Testament**

**The Bible has wise sayings to help people
live in the right way day by day.**

7 Let's look at
Songs

Sometimes, when you are happy,
you want to sing and dance for joy.
Sometimes, when you're miserable,
a sad song seems to understand.

In the Bible are songs written long ago
by people who loved God.
There are happy songs
and sad songs.

*Let everything
in all the world
sing praise to God:
the sun, the moon,
the stars, the skies,
the land, the sea,
the plants, the animals,
and all the people—
for God made them all.
God is great.*

**From the songbook of the Bible, the
book called Psalms**

*As a deer longs for a drink of cool water
so I long for you, dear God . . .
I am so sad, so unhappy
and I don't know why—
but I will look to God to help me,
God the rescuer,
and then I will be able to sing
happy songs again.*

Another of the Psalms

For hundreds of years, the people who love God have used these songs to tell God what they're thinking and how they're feeling.

The Bible has songs to sing to God—songs for happy times, sad times and all times!

8 Let's look at
Prayers

It's good to have a friend
you can really talk to—
someone who will listen
to whatever you have to say;
someone who will be glad to hear
your good news;
someone who will stay close
when you're lonely;
someone who is strong when you
need help.

The people who love God
talk to him as a friend:
they say prayers.
In the Bible there are prayers
by people who lived long ago,
who loved God
and spent time talking to him.

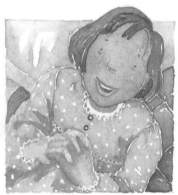

Dear God,
You give me all I need.
You guide me in what I should do.
You always keep me safe.
How happy I am to spend time
with you.
From the book of Psalms

The Bible has prayers that help
people learn how to talk to God.

9 Let's look at

Life stories

What makes people famous?
Why do crowds rush to see them?
What is their life story?
Who will tell you about them?

In the New Testament part of the Bible
there are four stories about a famous person:
Jesus Christ.
Each story is a bit different,
because it was written by a different person:
Matthew, Mark, Luke, and John.
They wrote down the things Jesus said about God
and about how people should live.
They told the stories of how he healed people.
They remembered the day he was put to death
and the day he came to life again.
They remembered the day he went back to heaven.
They wanted to spread the good news
that Jesus was God's Son,
who came to live in the world
to make people God's friends again.

Before he went back to heaven
Jesus said to the group of his special friends,
"Go to all people everywhere.
Tell them about me,
so they can follow me
and live as God wants them to."

From the very end of the book Matthew wrote about Jesus

The Bible tells people about Jesus, so that they can believe in him too.

10 Let's look at
Adventures

It's exciting to read about great adventures
of people setting off to do great deeds.

The book of Acts in the Bible
tells the story of the followers of Jesus,
and their adventures.
God gave them the courage
to spread Jesus' message of new life
to many different countries.

They faced many dangers:
they were put in prison,
shipwrecked,
left with very little money...
but they were so sure that
God was helping them
that they carried on with
their great task with joy.
Their message—
the Christian faith—
changed the world.

**The Bible tells the story of
the first Christians and
shows how God helped
them spread the news
about Jesus.**

11 Let's look at
Letters

Why write a letter?
There are thank-you-very-much letters,
missing-you letters,
wish-you-were-here letters,
get-well-soon letters,
I've-got-great-news letters.
Isn't it wonderful to get a letter from a friend?

The followers of Jesus
wrote letters to the new groups of Christians:
thanking them for their help;
saying how much they missed them;
asking for prayers for people who were ill;
and telling them more about Jesus
and how they should live.

You are the people of God.
He loved you
and chose you for his own.
So you must be kind
to one another.
Be patient,
and forgive each other
just as God has forgiven you.

From a letter written by a Christian leader
named Paul to the Christians in the ancient
town of Colossae

The Bible has letters written to new Christians that explain how Jesus wants them to live.

12 Let's look at
Light in the dark

Imagine being in the dark,
not knowing where to go
or what to do,
bumping into things by mistake,
getting hurt,
getting into danger.

The Bible says
that what God has told people
about himself
and about how to live
is like a light in the dark:
it tells people how to see their way
safely through life.

Dear God,
What you say is a lamp to
guide me
and a light for my path.

From Psalm 119

The things that God tells people in the Bible can help guide them when life is difficult, like a light in the dark.

13 Let's look at
Answers

When you have a problem,
you feel stuck.
But when you have an answer,
you know what to do.

Many people,
who wonder what life is for
and how they should live it,
find answers in the Bible.
There they read
that God made them,
that God loves them,
and that God sent Jesus
to make them his friends,
so they could be happy
forever.

Since you were a child
you have studied the scriptures.
They have made you truly wise
so that you understand
how Jesus can help you
if you believe in him.

From the letter that a Christian leader named Paul wrote to a young Christian named Timothy. The Bible is sometimes called "Scripture".

The Bible teaches people how Jesus can help them to be really happy.

What is the Bible?

1   The Bible explains why the world exists: because God made it just as he wanted.

2   The Bible tells people about God's promises to care for them and for the world.

3   The Bible tells the story of God and his people, and it shows how much God loves everyone.

4   The Bible gives God's rules for living a really happy life.

5   The Bible tells people how important it is to remember God.

6   The Bible has wise sayings to help people live in the right way day by day.

7   The Bible has songs to sing to God—songs for happy times, sad times, and all times!

8   The Bible has prayers that help people learn how to talk to God.

9   The Bible tells people about Jesus, so that they can believe in him too.

10 The Bible tells the story of the first Christians and shows how God helped them spread the news about Jesus.

11 The Bible has letters written to new Christians that explain how Jesus wants them to live.

12 The things that God tells people in the Bible can help guide them when life is difficult, like a light in the dark.

13 The Bible teaches people how Jesus can help them to be really happy.